MW00893832

Copyright © 2024 by Jasper Todd

All rights reserved.

No portion of this book may be reproduced in any form without written permission from the publisher or author, except as permitted by U.S. copyright law.

TABLE OF CONTENTS

GETTING STARTED

BEGINNER LEVEL

INTERMEDIATE LEVEL

ADVANCED LEVEL

READY TO TAKE YOUR LEARNING TO A WHOLE NEW LEVEL

GET THE **ULTIMATE YO-YO VIDEO COURSE** FOR KIDS!

EXCLUSIVE TO AMAZON CUSTOMERS!

YOU'LL RECIEVE:

 LIFETIME ACCESS TO OVER **40** **PROFESSIONAL VIDEO TUTORIALS!**

 **DOWNLOADABLE** PDFs FOR EVERY TRICK!

 **EXTRA BONUSES** (SLOWMO VIDEOS & REVERSED VIDEOS)

SCAN THE QR CODE TO GET INSTANT ACCESS

AND MORE!

SEE YOU ON THE INSIDE!

WELCOME TO THE WORLD OF YOYO!

HEY THERE, FUTURE YOYO MASTERS!

Welcome to the amazing world of yoyoing, where we're going to **SPIN, FLIP**, and **FLY** through some of the coolest tricks out there!

We'll kick things off with fun moves like **WALKING THE DOG**, then take you on an adventure with **AROUND THE WORLD**.

READY TO SHOOT FOR THE STARS?

Get excited for **SKY ROCKET!** You'll even learn mind-blowing tricks like **SPLIT THE ATOM** and mesmerize your friends with the famous **DNA TRICK!**

Yoyoing is not just about performing tricks—it's a **FUN** and **EXCITING WAY TO EXPRESS YOURSELF** and show off your unique style!

Whether you've never picked up a yoyo before or you've tried a few tricks, this trick book is your **TICKET TO LEARNING THE BEAUTIFUL ART OF YOYOING.**

Are you ready to learn how to **SPIN**, do **SUPER COOL TRICKS**, and **WOW** your friends? Go grab your new, shiny yoyo, and let's kick off this epic yoyo adventure together!

But before we dive into tricks, let's **LEARN** a bit more about the yoyos themselves and get you set up for success!

TYPES OF YOYO

THERE ARE MANY SHAPES AND SIZES OF YOYOS BUT THERE ARE ONLY **TWO COMMON SHAPES** YOU ONLY NEED TO REMEMBER.

1 Classic Imperial shape

This one's been around forever, and it's a favorite for beginners and yoyo legends alike. Your parents (or even your grandparents!) probably had one of these. It's **super easy** to hold and **perfect for starting out**.

2 Butterfly Shape

Modern yoyo players love this one because it's perfect for all kinds of **advanced string tricks**. Its wide shape helps the string stay in place, which reduces the friction, allowing your yoyo to spin much longer!

ANATOMY OF A YOYO

What makes a yoyo spin so smoothly?
Let's break it down!

A YOYO WORKS A LOT **LIKE A GYROSCOPE**, AND ITS DESIGN HAS IMPROVED OVER TIME TO HELP YOU PULL OFF MORE AND MORE AMAZING TRICKS. HERE ARE THE KEY PARTS THAT MAKE A MODERN YOYO WORK SO WELL:

This small but super important piece **helps the yoyo spin** for a really long time, giving you plenty of time to pull off awesome tricks while it's still spinning.

BALL BEARING

This is the part that connects everything together. It runs through the ball bearing and spacers to hold everything in place.

AXLE

SPACERS

These little parts hold the ball bearing in place, making sure everything stays steady and balanced.

MAIN BODY

This is the yoyo itself— the two halves that come together to create the perfect spinning toy!

Put all these parts together, and you've got a yoyo ready for some serious spinning action!

But wait—don't forget about the yoyo string!

We'll show you how to attach it in just a moment so your yoyo is fully ready to go.

SETTING UP YOUR YOYO

NOW THAT YOU KNOW THE PARTS, IT'S TIME TO SET UP YOUR YOYO! **IF YOUR YOYO IS ALREADY ASSEMBLED, SKIP AHEAD,** BUT IF IT'S IN PIECES, DON'T WORRY—WE'LL SHOW YOU HOW TO PUT IT ALL TOGETHER.

STEP 1 Starting with the half that has the *axle already attached*, put the *spacer* through the axle, making sure that the *flat side touches the main body*.

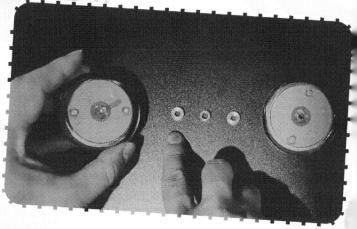

Next, slide on the *ball bearing*, and then the *other spacer*.

 BE SURE THAT THE FLAT SIDE OF THE *SPACER DOESN'T TOUCH THE BEARING.* NOW SCREW ON THE OTHER HALF OF THE MAIN BODY. MAKE SURE IT'S NICE AND TIGHT.

STEP 2

Next step is to attach the string to the yoyo.

Take the string and untwist the end of it using your thumb and fingers to pull the string apart and create a loop.

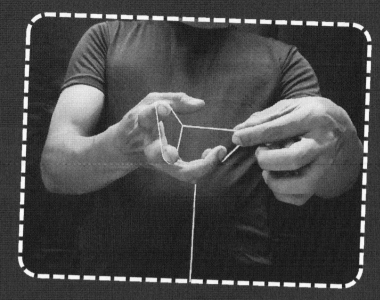

STEP 3

Now put the loop through the yoyo then retwist the string.

 STEP 4

After that, place the yoyo on the floor near where your feet are while holding the string in your hand.

Measure your string to **at least five inches above your belly button**.

Tie it into a loop knot then cut off the rest of the string that we don't need using a pair of scissors.

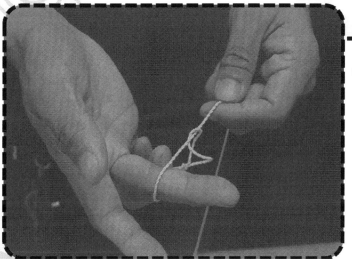

STEP **5** Now, time to attach the string to your finger.

Take the string coming down from the knot and pass it through the loop knot by pulling it.

If you do it this way, you'll have another loop that is adjustable.

Next, insert your middle finger right into the middle of the loop. Tighten it down right in between your first and second knuckle.

WINDING UP YOUR YOYO

HAVING TROUBLE GETTING YOUR YOYO TO WIND UP? THAT'S OKAY—HERE'S THE TRICK!

 1 Hold the yoyo with your index finger on top.

 2 Wrap the string around your finger once, then wind the string around the yoyo 3 to 5 times.

 3 Pull your finger out, and wind the rest of the string.

HOW TO HOLD AND SPIN YOUR YOYO

YOU'RE ALL SET UP AND READY FOR YOUR FIRST SPIN! LET'S MAKE SURE YOU'RE HOLDING THE YOYO THE RIGHT WAY

HOW TO HOLD:

With your **palm facing up**, make sure the string goes over the top of the yoyo.

This way, the yoyo will roll off your hand when you throw it.

If the string is coming from the bottom of the yoyo, flip it around, or you won't have control when you try to spin it.

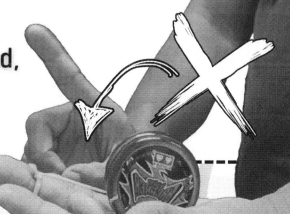

18

HOW TO SPIN:

1 Make sure you are holding the yoyo the right way and then curl up your arm, as if you are showing off your big strong muscles!

2 Now, throw your arm out and let the yoyo roll off your hand, aiming downwards.

3 When the yoyo reaches the end of the string, flip your hand over and watch the yoyo spin!

4 To bring it back, give the string a slight tug upwards.

HANDY TIP:

TRY THROWING THE YOYO WITH MORE POWER– IT WILL SPIN FOR A MUCH LONGER TIME, GIVING YOU PLENTY OF TIME TO TRY SOME COOL TRICKS!

SAFETY FIRST!

BEFORE WE KICK OFF AND START SPINNING, LET'S PAUSE FOR A QUICK SAFETY REMINDER:

 Make sure to keep a good distance from other people to avoid accidentally hitting anyone while you're yoyoing.

 Play in a spacious area to avoid breaking things around you.

THERE YOU HAVE IT – SAFETY BRIEFING DONE! NOW YOU'RE READY TO START YOUR YOYO ADVENTURE!

YOYO COURSE TRICK LEVELS

NOW, FOR THE FUN PART! IN THIS BOOK, YOU'LL DISCOVER **30 SUPER COOL YOYO TRICKS** THAT YOU CAN EASILY LEARN BY FOLLOWING OUR SIMPLE STEP-BY-STEP INSTRUCTIONS.

THESE TRICKS ARE DIVIDED INTO **3 LEVELS:**

BEGINNER LEVEL ★

We'll start with the easiest tricks to learn. Even though they're simple, they're still super impressive!

INTERMEDIATE LEVEL ★★

We'll crank up the difficulty with some mind-blowing tricks like the Brain Twister, the UFO, and the Boomerang!

ADVANCED LEVEL ★★★

This is where the real yoyo magic begins, with incredible string tricks and yoyo combos.

RARR!

AND EVEN AFTER ALL OF THAT, WE'VE STILL GOT MORE EXCITING TIPS AND TRICKS TO SHOW YOU. READY? LET'S GO!

TRICK NO. 01
GRAVITY PULL

WE'RE KICKING OFF THE SHOW WITH THE EASIEST TRICK IN THE BOOK—THE GRAVITY PULL. IT'S **QUICK, EFFORTLESS,** BUT **OH-SO-SATISFYING!**

STEP 1
Start by curling your arm up like you're showing off your big bicep muscles.

STEP 2
Now, straighten your arm out and release the yoyo downward from your hand.

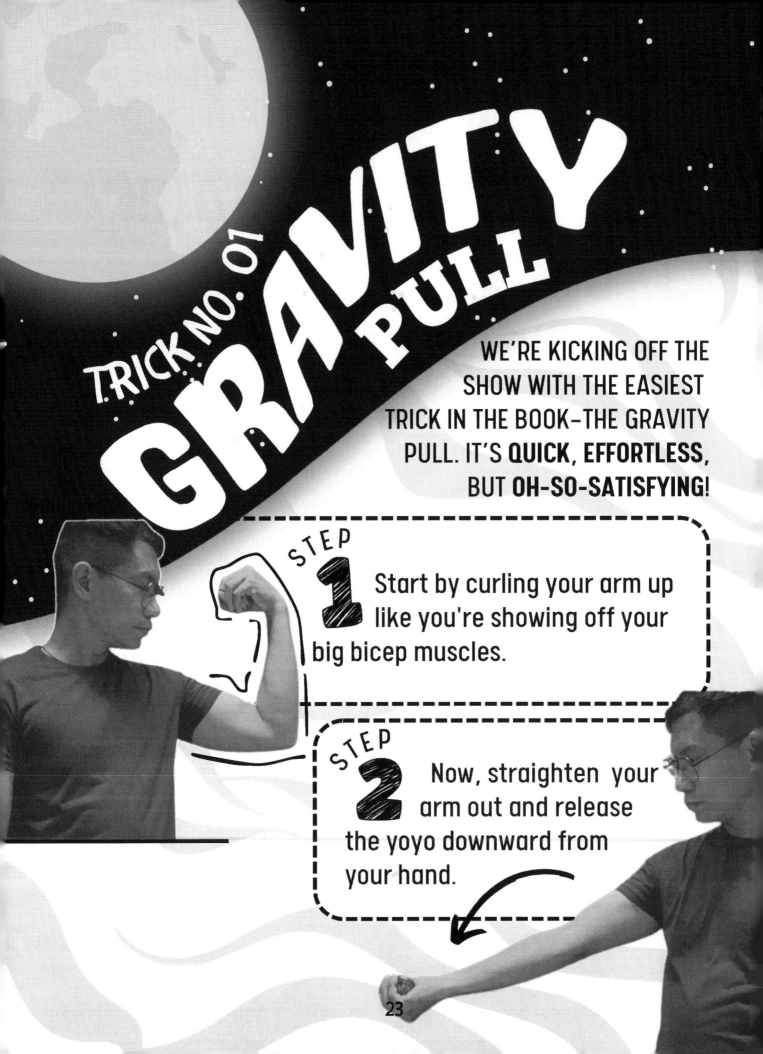

TRICK NO. 01 GRAVITY PULL

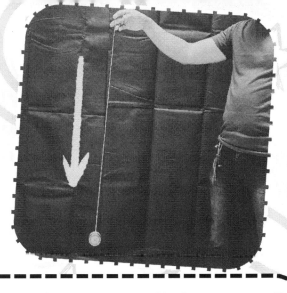

STEP 3 Let the yoyo roll down until it reaches the end of the string.

STEP 4 As soon as the yoyo reaches the bottom, quickly tug the string and catch the yoyo back in your hand.

SUPER QUICK AND EASY, RIGHT? YOU CAN EVEN DO THIS WITH YOUR EYES CLOSED!

TRICK NO. 02
THE LONG SLEEPER

THIS NEXT TRICK IS SIMILAR TO GRAVITY PULL. THE ONLY DIFFERENCE IS YOU **LET THE YOYO SPIN** AT THE END OF THE STRING FOR **A FEW SECONDS**.

STEP 1 Start off by curling your arm up like you're showing off your muscles.

STEP 2 Start off by curling your arm up like you're showing off your muscles.

THE LONG SLEEPER

TRICK NO. 02

STEP **3** Once the yoyo reaches the end of the string, let it spin there at the bottom for at least three seconds.

STEP **4** After that, with your palm facing down, give the string a slight tug to return the yoyo to your hand.

And that's the Long Sleeper!

TRY RECORDING YOUR SPINNING TIME. I CHALLENGE YOU TO SEE IF YOU CAN DO MORE THAN A MINUTE!

26

WALK THE DOG

HERE'S A CLASSIC YOYO TRICK THAT EVERYONE KNOWS–**WALK THE DOG.** IT'S A TIMELESS FAVORITE!

STEP 1

Start the trick by doing a **Long Sleeper**.

STEP 2

Carefully let the yoyo touch the ground.

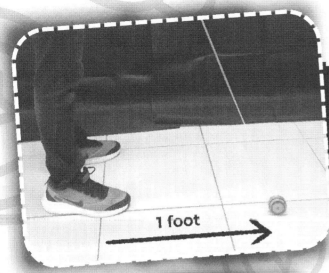

1 foot

Let it walk at least a foot along the ground.

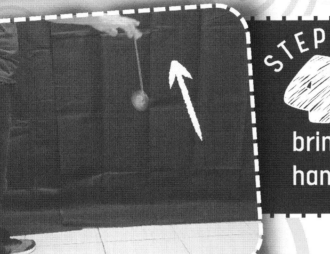

STEP 4

Before the yoyo runs out of spin, tug the string and bring the yoyo back to your hand.

PRO TIP:

MAKE SURE YOU **DO A STRONG LONG SLEEPER THROW** SO THE YOYO HAS ENOUGH SPIN, AS THE FRICTION ON THE FLOOR WILL SLOW IT DOWN.

THE FORWARD PASS

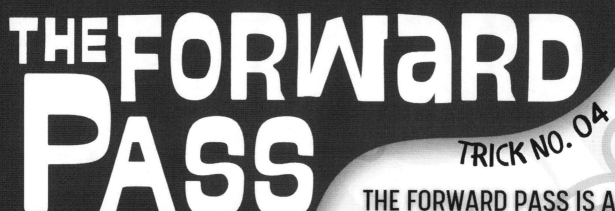

THE FORWARD PASS IS A SUPER QUICK AND EASY TRICK. YOU CAN EVEN DO IT WITH YOUR EYES CLOSED TOO!

STEP 1 Place your hand at the side of your body.

STEP 2 Swing your arm forward and release the yoyo in front of you.

STEP 3 When the yoyo reaches the end of the string, it will automatically return to your hand.

STEP 4 Catch the yoyo with your palm facing upward, and you've finished the trick!

IT'S JUST LIKE **GRAVITY PULL**, BUT YOU'RE **THROWING THE YOYO FORWARD** INSTEAD OF DOWNWARD.

SAFETY TIP!

ALWAYS MAKE SURE YOU HAVE PLENTY OF SPACE AROUND YOU WHEN DOING TRICKS LIKE THIS!

TRICK NO. 05
BREAK AWAY

HERE'S ANOTHER QUICK AND EASY TRICK CALLED **BREAK AWAY**.

IT'S ONE OF THE MOST FUNDAMENTAL YOYO TRICKS BECAUSE MANY OTHER TRICKS START WITH THIS EXACT MOVE.

STEP 1
Make a muscle with your arm, but turn it to the side.

STEP 2
Throw the yoyo and swing it in front of you in an arch.

STEP 3
As soon as the yoyo reaches shoulder height, give it a slight tug and catch the yoyo with your palm facing upward.

PRACTICE BREAK AWAY, AS YOU'LL BE USING THIS MOVE IN ADVANCED TRICKS LATER ON!

TRICK NO. 06
ST★R

TIME TO PERFORM OUR FIRST PICTURE YOYO TRICK! WE'RE GOING TO CREATE A STAR.

STEP 1
Start with a strong Long Sleeper

STEP 2
Form a Star with the string by wrapping it around your fingers.

REMEMBER THIS PATTERN!

CONFUSED? DON'T WORRY! I'LL TEACH YOU STEP-BY-STEP IN THE NEXT PAGE

PRACTICE WITHOUT THE YOYO SPINNING AT FIRST.

YOU CAN USE YOUR OTHER HAND TO HELP

HERE'S A STEP-BY-STEP ON HOW TO MASTER THE PATTERN!

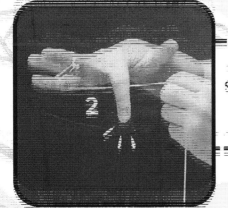

STEP 1 Start by placing the string above your pinky finger

STEP 2 Then place the string under and over your index finger

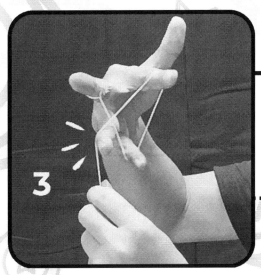

STEP 3

After that, place it **over your ring finger**, then your **thumb**.

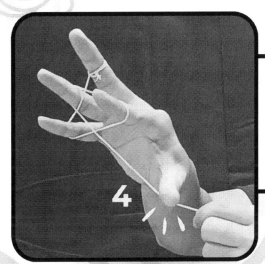

STEP 4

Finally, hang the string **over your middle finger**, and hey presto! You've now formed a **STAR!**

ONCE YOU'VE MASTERED FORMING THE STAR, TRY IT WITH THE YOYO SPINNING. HAVE FUN WITH IT, AND I'LL SEE YOU AT THE NEXT TRICK.

SKY ROCKET

NEXT UP, WE'RE GOING TO EXPLORE THE MILKY WAY WITH THE AWESOME SKY ROCKET!

! BE CAREFUL: MAKE SURE YOU'RE IN A SPACE WITH A HIGH CEILING, OR BETTER YET, GO OUTSIDE.

STEP **1** Start the trick with a **Long Sleeper**.

STEP **2** **Remove** the string from your finger.

STEP 3 Now, give the string a slight tug and let the yoyo fly high above your head, like it's reaching for the sky!

 STEP 4 Catch the yoyo as it falls back down.

THIS TRICK IS PERFECT AS A FINISHING MOVE WHENEVER YOU PERFORM YOYO TRICKS. SIMPLE BUT FLASHY!

ROCK THE BABY

YOU CAN PRACTICE THIS TRICK WITHOUT SPINNING THE YOYO AT FIRST

STEP 1
Grab the string from your throw hand about a third of the way up with your other hand.

Then fold just like this

STEP 2
Fold it and **pinch** the other part of the string.

STEP 3 Create a **triangle shape** with the string to form a cradle.

STEP 4 The yoyo will sit in the **center of the cradle**.

STEP 5 Swing the yoyo back and **forth at least three times**

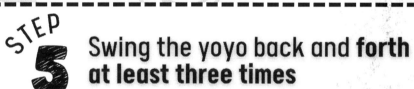

STEP 6 **Release the string**, let the yoyo **drop**, and **tug** the string to bring it back to your hand

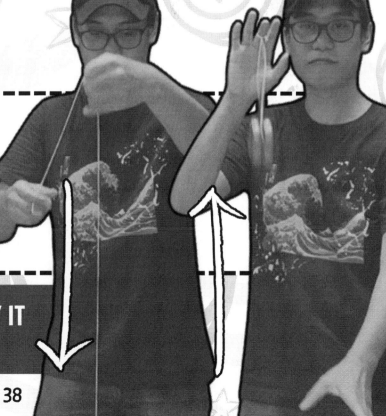

WHEN YOU'RE CONFIDENT, TRY IT WHILE THE YOYO IS SPINNING!

ELEVATOR

STEP 1 Start with a **hard Long Sleeper.**

STEP 2 Use the **index finger** of your other hand to catch the string.

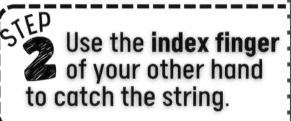

STEP 3 **Lower** your throwhand and **raise** the other hand

STEP 4 Put the string into the **gap** of the yoyo.

STEP 5

Pull the string with your throwhand, and the yoyo will ride up like an elevator!

STEP 6

You can also move the yoyo back **down and up again.**

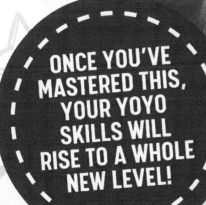

ONCE YOU'VE MASTERED THIS, YOUR YOYO SKILLS WILL RISE TO A WHOLE NEW LEVEL!

AROUND WORLD

TRICK NO. 10

STEP 1 Start with a **Forward Pass**

STEP 2 When the yoyo reaches the end of the string, let it swing in a **circular motion** instead of catching it right away

41

YOU CAN ALSO PRACTICE THIS WITHOUT THE YOYO SPINNING. TRY MAKING MORE THAN ONE ROTATION AS YOU IMPROVE!

CONGRATULATIONS!

YOU'VE MASTERED THE BEGINNER LEVEL!

YOU'VE LEARNED SOME IMPRESSIVE TRICKS, AND BY NOW, YOU'VE GOT A SOLID FOUNDATION TO TAKE YOUR YOYO SKILLS TO THE NEXT STAGE.

BUT THE FUN DOESN'T STOP HERE!

AS WE MOVE INTO THE

INTERMEDIATE LEVEL

WE'LL START DIVING INTO MORE INTRICATE AND EXCITING TRICKS THAT WILL CHALLENGE YOUR **COORDINATION**, **TIMING**, AND **CREATIVITY**.

THESE TRICKS WILL BUILD ON WHAT YOU'VE ALREADY LEARNED, INTRODUCING NEW MOVES AND TECHNIQUES THAT WILL MAKE YOUR YOYOING EVEN MORE

MIND-BLOWING!

SO, GET READY TO STEP UP YOUR GAME AND AMAZE YOUR FRIENDS AS WE MOVE INTO THE **INTERMEDIATE TRICKS**-THIS IS WHERE THE **REAL ADVENTURE BEGINS!**

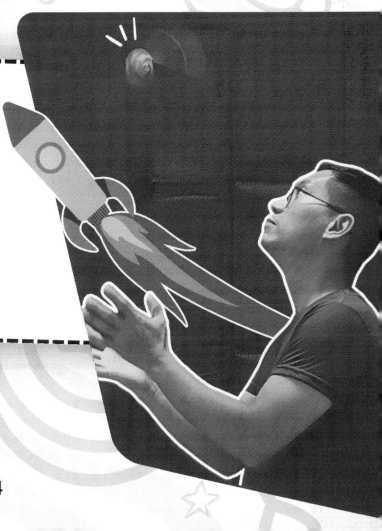

DIZZY BABY
TRICK NO. 11

HERE'S A **VARIATION OF THE ROCK THE BABY** TRICK. INSTEAD OF JUST ROCKING THE YOYO BACK AND FORTH, YOU'LL **SPIN IT AROUND INSIDE THE CRADLE.**

TO PRACTICE, TRY IT FIRST WITHOUT THE YOYO SPINNING

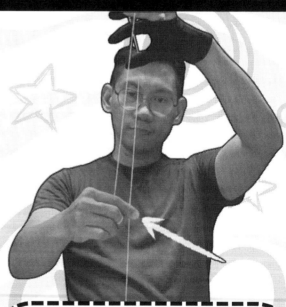

STEP 1 Form the **triangular-shaped cradle** with the string.

STEP 2 Make sure the string **does not cross-over** itself to avoid a knot

45

STEP 3

Spin the yoyo around inside the cradle at least **three times.**

STEP 4

To finish, drop the yoyo down slowly and give it a tug to return it to your hand.

ONCE YOU GET THE HANG OF IT, TRY DOING IT WITH THE YOYO SPINNING!

EIFFEL TOWER

SINCE WE'VE TRAVELED AROUND THE WORLD, LET'S VISIT PARIS AND CREATE THE EIFFEL TOWER!

PRACTICE THIS TRICK FIRST WITHOUT THE YOYO SPINNING:

STEP 1 Place your other hand in **front of the string.**

STEP 2 Using your **thumb and index finger** on both hands, form a **rectangle** shape with the string.

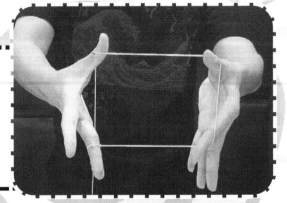

47

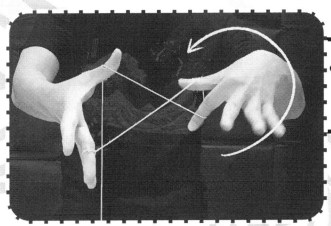

STEP 3 **Twist the string** with your other hand

STEP 4 Pinch the string that's hanging.

pinch this

STEP 5 When you pull the string, the tower will start to form. Adjust it to make the tower look perfect.

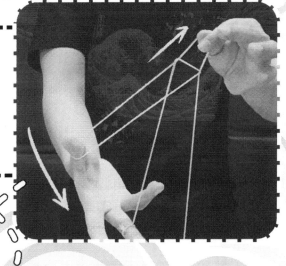

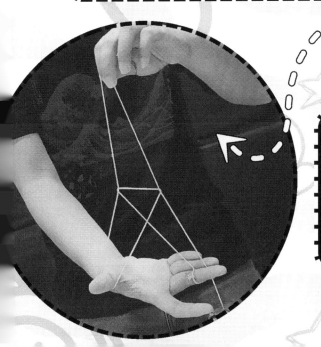

IF YOU DO THE TRICK WHILE THE YOYO IS SPINNING, SIMPLY DROP THE YOYO SLOWLY AND CATCH IT TO FINISH.

TRICK NO. 13
PINWHEEL

CAN'T STOP SPINNING? YOU'LL LOVE THE PINWHEEL TRICK! IT TAKES A LITTLE TIME TO MASTER, BUT IT'S TONS OF FUN.

STEP 1 Start with a **long sleeper**

STEP 2 Grab the string and **pinch** it about 5-7 inches from the yoyo.

STEP 3

Spin the yoyo around in a **pinwheel motion 3 times**

STEP 4

To finish, drop the yoyo down

STEP 5

Then **catch** it in your hand

YOUR FRIENDS AND FAMILY WILL BE IMPRESSED WHEN YOU SHOW THEM THE PINWHEEL!

TRICK NO. 14
TWO-HANDED STAR

REMEMBER THE **STAR TRICK FROM THE BEGINNER LEVEL**?

THIS TRICK IS SIMILAR, **BUT BIGGER!** IT'S A LITTLE TRICKIER SINCE YOU'LL NEED BOTH HANDS.

REMEMBER THIS PATTERN!

PRACTICE WITHOUT THE YOYO SPINNING AT FIRST:

 STEP 1 Place the string over your **other hand's thumb**.

STEP Place the string under and over your throwhand's **pinky finger**.

STEP 3 Place it over your other hand's **index finger**.

STEP 4 Place it over your **throwhand's thumb**

STEP 5 Hang the string over your throwhand's **middle finger**.

YOU'VE NOW FORMED A BIGGER STAR!

UFO

TIME TO BLAST OFF INTO SPACE WITH THE UFO TRICK!

THERE ARE TWO WAYS TO START THIS TRICK: THROWING THE YOYO TO THE **RIGHT SIDE** OR THE **LEFT SIDE**.

LET'S LEARN BOTH. READY?

RIGHT SIDE

STEP 1 Throw the yoyo **diagonally** to the **right side**, away from your body

STEP 2

Quickly grab the string a few inches from the yoyo.

STEP 3

Let the yoyo spin horizontally, **like a UFO.**

STEP 4

To finish, **pop the yoyo up** and catch it in your hand.

STEP 1 Throw the yoyo **diagonally** to the **left side**, away from your body

STEP 2 **Quickly grab** the string a few inches from the yoyo.

STEP 3 Let the yoyo spin **horizontally**.

Grab

STEP 4 After a few seconds, **pop the yoyo up** and **catch it** in your hand.

PICK WHICHEVER SIDE FEELS EASIEST FOR YOU, AND YOU'LL BE DOING THE UFO IN NO TIME!

UNDER MOUNT

NOW IT'S TIME FOR A **BASIC STRING LANDING TRICK!** **THE UNDERMOUNT** MIGHT LOOK TRICKY, BUT IT'S VERY SIMPLE ONCE YOU KNOW HOW TO DO IT.

STEP 1 Start with a **hard throw** for a **Long Sleeper**.

STEP 2 Swing the yoyo **backward toward yourself.**

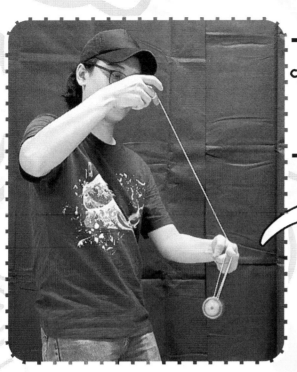

STEP 3 Use your **other hand's index finger** to land the yoyo **on the string**.

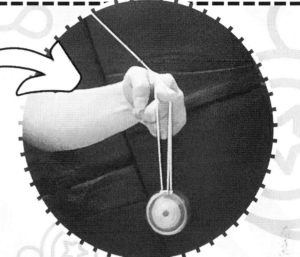

STEP 4 To finish, **reverse** the movement to dismount the yoyo and return it to your hand.

FOR EASY MODE

A BUTTERFLY-SHAPED YOYO WILL MAKE IT EASIER TO LAND THE YOYO ON THE STRING!

TRICK NO. 17
TRAPEZE

ALSO KNOWN AS **_"THE MAN ON THE FLYING TRAPEZE,"_** THIS TRICK IS A MUST-KNOW FOR EVERY YOYO MASTER!

STEP 1 Start with a **Breakaway throw.**

STEP 2 As the yoyo swings, use your **other hand's index finger to land** the yoyo on the string.

THIS ONE'S SIMILAR TO UNDERMOUNT, BUT REVERSED

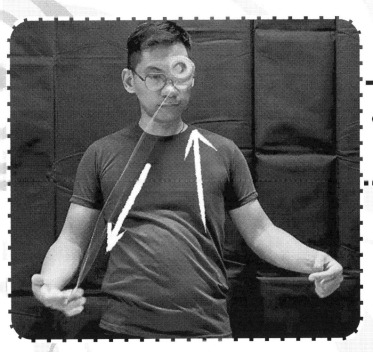

STEP 3 To finish, pop the yoyo up and catch it in your hand.

YOU CAN PRACTICE THIS TRICK BY DOING A **LONG SLEEPER TO THE SIDE** AND **ESTIMATING HOW THE YOYO WILL LAND ON THE STRING.**

BRAIN TWISTER

TRICK NO. 18

HERE'S A SUPER FUN TRICK—THE BRAIN TWISTER!
IT MAY BE A BIT CHALLENGING AT FIRST, BUT
ONCE YOU GET IT, IT'S VERY SATISFYING.

STEP 1 Start with a **Long Sleeper.**

STEP 2 **Pull the yoyo above** using your other hand's index finger

Then **put the string into the gap of the yoyo** with your throwhand, similar to the first step of the Elevator trick.

STEP 3 Bring your throwhand up into the yoyo, creating an **UNDERMOUNT**

(but with the throwhand below your other hand)

STEP 4

Push your throwhand into the string to make the yoyo go around in a circular motion.

REPEAT THIS AT LEAST TWO TIMES, OR AS MANY TIMES AS YOU LIKE!

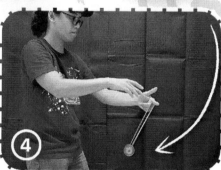

STEP 5

To finish, dismount the yoyo and catch it in your hand.

HERE'S A TIP:

A **STRONG LONG SLEEPER** WILL GIVE YOU ENOUGH SPIN POWER TO COMPLETE THIS TRICK!

STOP AND DASH

IT'S TIME TO **STOP... AND DASH** INTO THIS NEXT TRICK! IT'S SUPER COOL AND SURE TO IMPRESS.

STEP 1 Start with a **Long Sleeper.**

STEP 2 Do the first few steps of the **Brain Twister** to create an **Undermount.**

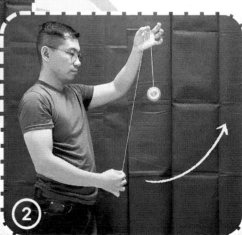

STEP 3

Both hands should now be at the **same level.**

STEP 4

Tug the yoyo up and **catch** it with both hands.

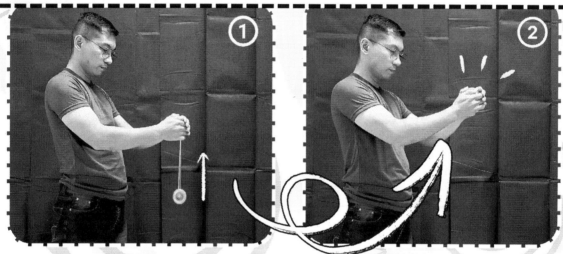

STEP 5

To **spin the yoyo again,** place your throwhand below with the palm facing upward and your other hand above.

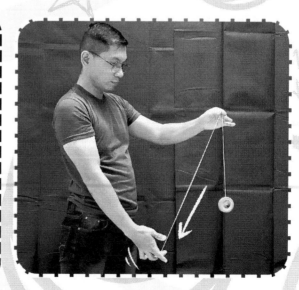

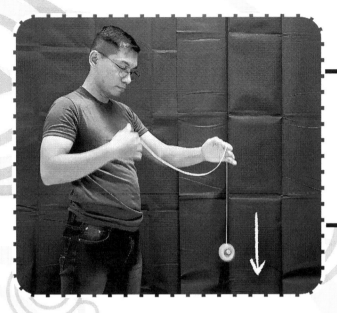

STEP **6** **Pull your throwhand down** to release the yoyo.

STEP **7** With the yoyo spinning again, **drop it down and tug** the string to bring it back to your hand.

AFTER MASTERING THIS TRICK, WE'RE DASHING TO THE LAST STOP OF THE INTERMEDIATE LEVEL!

BOOMERANG

FOR THE FINAL TRICK OF THE INTERMEDIATE LEVEL, WE'RE THROWING IN THE BOOMERANG!

STEP 1 Start with a **Long Sleeper.**

STEP 2 Do the **Elevator trick** move.

STEP **3**

Bounce the yoyo off the front.

STEP **4**

The yoyo will bounce back to the string. Keep repeating this motion.

BOUNCE IT AS MANY TIMES AS YOU LIKE.

STEP **5**

To finish, **drop the yoyo and tug the string** to return it to your hand.

TIMING IS THE KEY TO THIS TRICK, SO TAKE YOUR TIME PRACTICING!

THAT CONCLUDES THE INTERMEDIATE LEVEL!

THINGS ARE ABOUT TO GET EVEN MORE EXCITING AS WE HEAD INTO THE

THE TRICKS WILL BE MORE CHALLENGING, BUT THEY'RE INCREDIBLY REWARDING ONCE YOU PULL THEM OFF.

READY FOR THE NEXT LEVEL?

WOOHOO

YOU MADE IT!

GREAT JOB ON COMPLETING

THE INTERMEDIATE LEVEL

BY NOW, YOU'VE MASTERED SOME IMPRESSIVE TRICKS THAT HAVE TAKEN YOUR YOYO SKILLS TO NEW HEIGHTS.

BUT NOW, IT'S TIME TO REALLY PUT YOUR ABILITIES TO THE TEST AS WE ENTER THE....

ADVANCED LEVEL

THESE TRICKS ARE GOING TO BE MORE COMPLEX AND DEMANDING, REQUIRING **PRECISION**, **CREATIVITY**, AND **PATIENCE**.

BUT DON'T WORRY - WITH EACH STEP, WE'LL GUIDE YOU THROUGH THE PROCESS.

YOU'RE ABOUT TO UNLOCK A WHOLE NEW LEVEL OF YOYO MASTERY THAT WILL LEAVE YOUR FRIENDS AND FAMILY IN AWE!

READY TO SHOW OFF YOUR ADVANCED YOYO SKILLS?

LET'S DIVE INTO THE ADVANCED LEVEL AND BEGIN WITH OUR FIRST TRICK, **MAGIC!**

MAGIC

LET'S DO SOMETHING SPECTACULAR FOR OUR FIRST TRICK IN ADVANCED LEVEL. YOU ARE GOING TO NEED A **LASER-FOCUSED CONCENTRATION** TO DO THIS MAGIC YOYO TRICK.

FIRST, **DO A LONG SLEEPER** OR YOU MAY START FIRST **WITHOUT THE YOYO SPINNING** TO PRACTICE THIS TRICK.

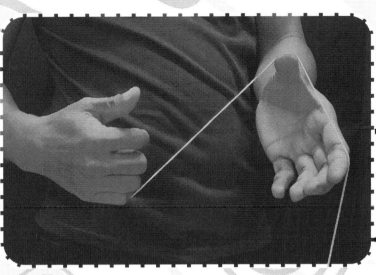

STEP 1 Place the string at **the back of your other hand.**

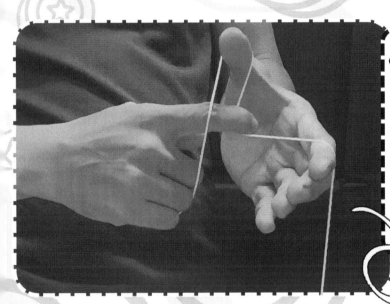

STEP 2 Using your throwhand's pointer finger, **grab the string at the gap** of your other hand's thumb and index finger.

MAKE SURE YOU GRAB IT UNDER THE STRING AT YOUR THROWHAND.

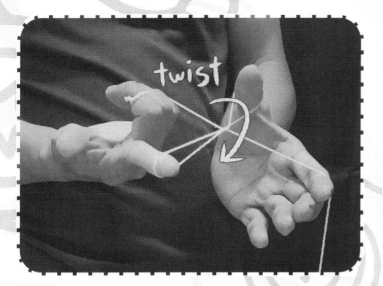
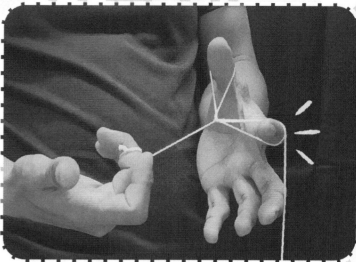

twist

STEP
3
Once you grab it, **twist it** to make a little loop, then **place it on the next finger**, the index finger of your other hand.

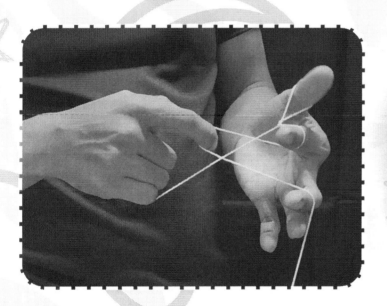

REPEAT STEPS 1-3 AGAIN, THIS TIME GRABBING THE STRING AT THE GAP BETWEEN YOUR INDEX AND MIDDLE FINGERS.

JUST GRAB, TWIST, AND PLACE THE STRING ON YOUR MIDDLE FINGER.

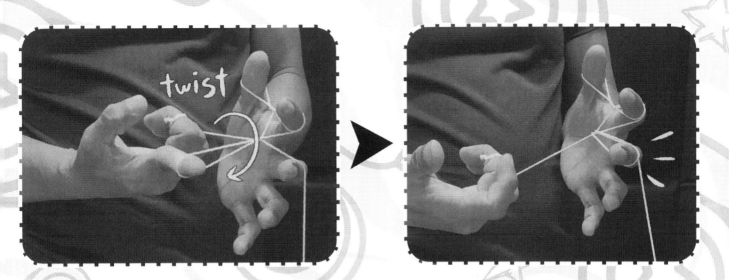

twist

After that, simply repeat the **same steps again** for your **ring finger** and **pinky**.

 **STEP 4** Once the string is placed on your fingers, **remove the string from your thumb.**

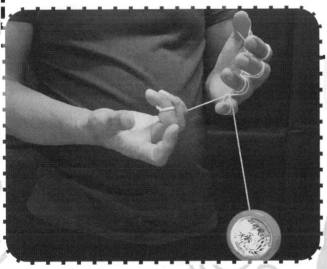

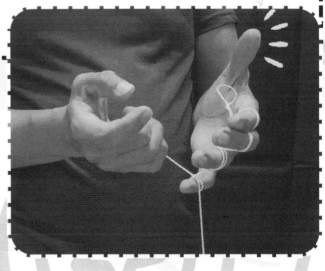

STEP 5 Then **pull the string** to undo the ties around your fingers.

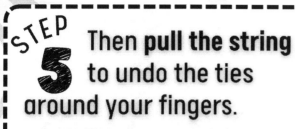

As you pull, the string will untie from your fingers, looking like **"MAGIC."**

↑ Pull

To finish, just **tug** the yoyo back to your hand.

FEEL FREE TO REVIEW THIS TRICK ANYTIME

KEEP TRACK OF THE STEPS, AND YOU'LL BE ABLE TO EASILY FOLLOW AND LEARN THE MAGIC YOYO TRICK IN NO TIME!

LINDY LOOP

THE NEXT TRICK IS A VARIATION OF TRAPEZE. YOU SIMPLY FLIP THE YOYO OVER AGAIN AFTER A TRAPEZE, AND YOU'VE JUST DONE A LINDY LOOP.

STEP 1 To begin, **throw a breakaway**, then perform a **Trapeze** trick.

STEP 2 After landing in a Trapeze, **flip the yoyo over** again to land in **another Trapeze.**

 ①

 ②

 ③

STEP 3 To end the trick, **reverse the movement** to bring the yoyo back to the regular Trapeze, then **pop the yoyo up** and catch it in your hand.

IT MAY LOOK SIMPLE, BUT IT'S IMPORTANT TO CONTROL THE YOYO WELL SO THAT THE SPIN TIME LASTS LONG ENOUGH TO DO THIS TRICK SMOOTHLY.

TRICK NO. 23
DOUBLE OR NOTHING

HERE'S ANOTHER IMPRESSIVE STRING TRICK: DOUBLE OR NOTHING, WHICH IS ALSO A VARIATION OF TRAPEZE.

 STEP 1 Start with a **throw of breakaway**.

 STEP 2 Catch the string with your **other hand's index finger**.

80

STEP 3 Instead of doing a Trapeze, **let the yoyo swing around** your throwhand's index finger.

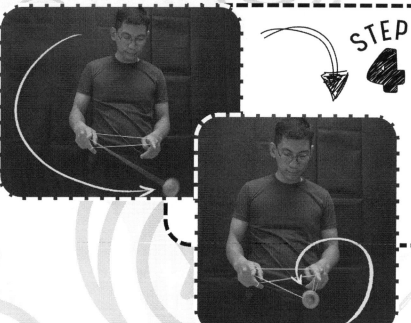

STEP 4 Then let the yoyo **swing around again,** reaching your other hand's index finger to land on the string.

TO DISMOUNT YOU HAVE 2 OPTIONS:

OPTION 1

Simply **pop the yoyo up and catch** it in your hand.

(This is the easiest.)

Drop the string from your throwhand's index finger

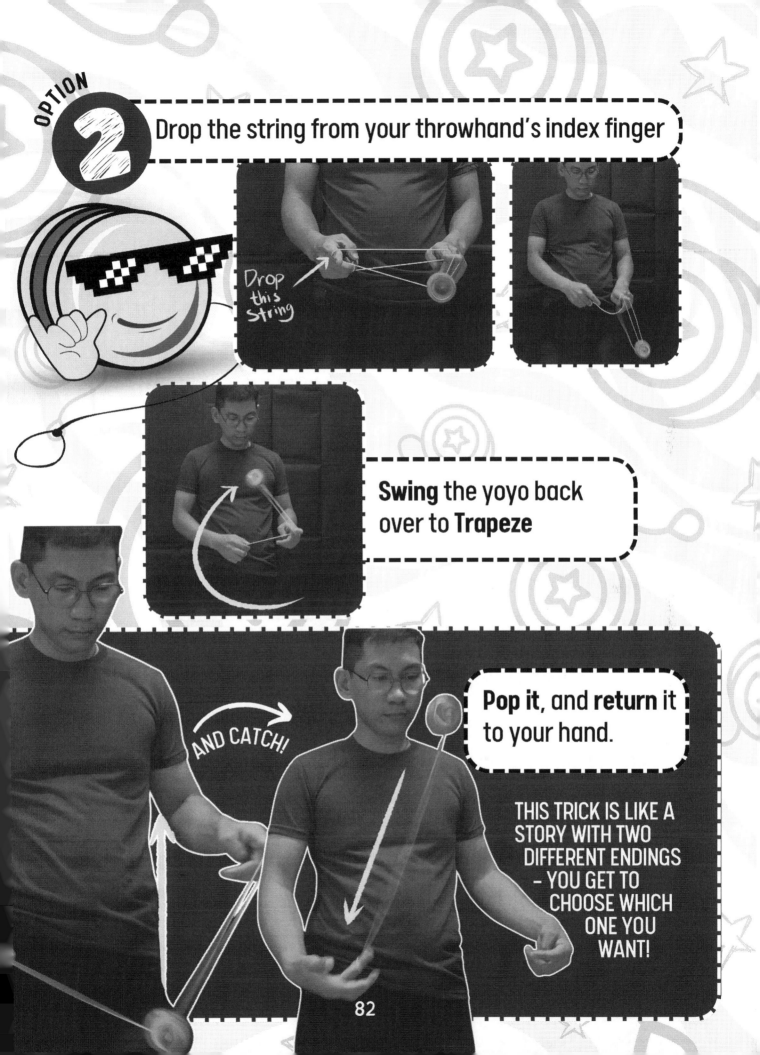

Drop this string

Swing the yoyo back over to **Trapeze**

AND CATCH!

Pop it, and **return** it to your hand.

THIS TRICK IS LIKE A STORY WITH TWO DIFFERENT ENDINGS – YOU GET TO CHOOSE WHICH ONE YOU WANT!

BARREL ROLL

LET'S STEP UP THE GAME WITH OUR NEXT TRICK. WE ARE GOING TO DO **THE BARREL ROLL!**

STEP 1
Begin the trick with **a long sleeper.**

STEP 2
Next, **perform a Brain Twister mount.**

But this time **move your throwhand over**, then behind your other hand.

LET'S TAKE A LOOK FROM A DIFFERENT ANGLE

STEP **3** Using the index finger of your throwhand, **pull the string** in front of you.

84

As you do the move, roll the yoyo to the back string, completing a single barrel roll.

TAKE A LOOK FROM A DIFFERENT ANGLE

FROM THIS, REPEAT THE MOVE AGAIN TWICE

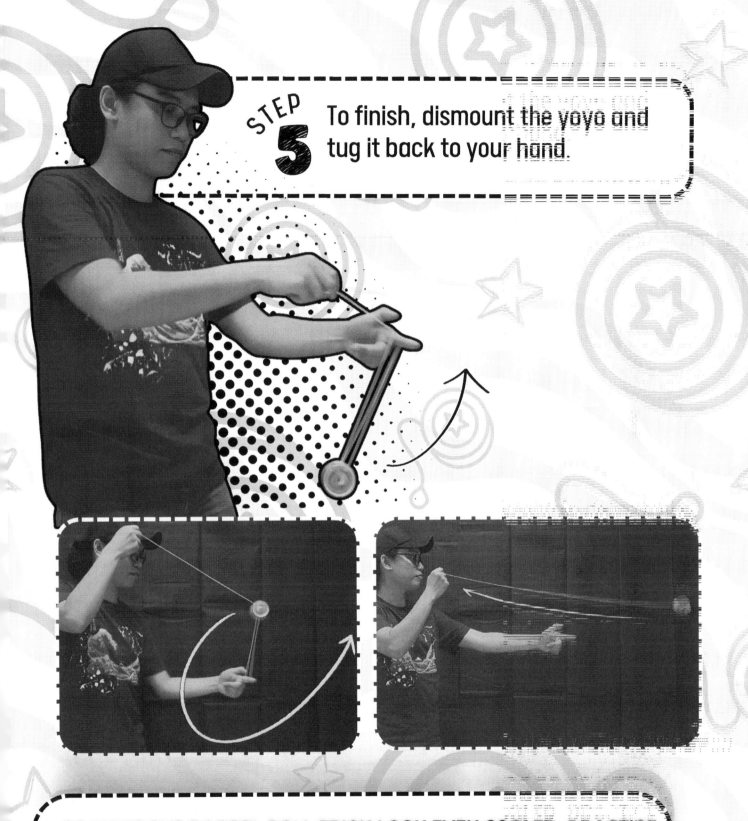

To finish, dismount the yoyo and tug it back to your hand.

TO MAKE THE BARREL ROLL TRICK LOOK EVEN **COOLER**, PRACTICE IT AGAIN AND AGAIN UNTIL YOU CAN DO IT **SMOOTHLY**, AND YOU WILL LOOK LIKE A **PRO YOYO MASTER!**

TRICK NO. 25
MOONSAULT BACK FLIP

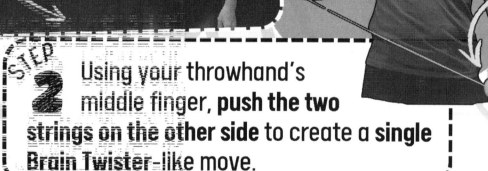

STEP 1 Start the trick with a **Trapeze.**

STEP 2 Using your throwhand's middle finger, **push the two strings on the other side** to create a **single Brain Twister**-like move.

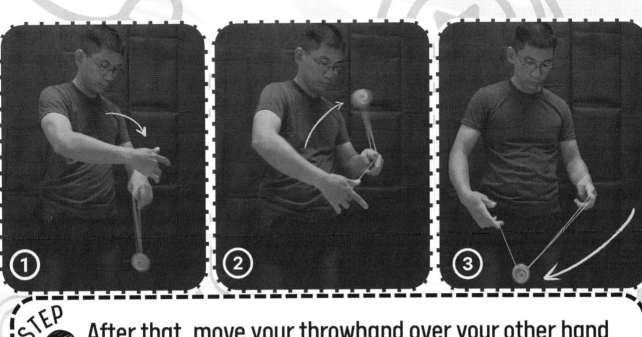

After that, move your throwhand over your other hand and roll the yoyo by swinging it back into a Trapeze.

STEP 4
Once you're in the Trapeze, simply **pop the yoyo up** and catch it to finish.

THE KEY TO LEARNING THE MOONSAULT BACK FLIP IS TO FIRST **DO IT SLOWLY**, PERFORMING EACH STEP ONE AT A TIME.

ONCE YOU GET THE GIST OF IT, TRY DOING THE TRICK IN ONE SMOOTH MOTION LIKE AN ABSOLUTE PRO!

SPLIT THE ATOM

ALRIGHT! THINGS ARE GETTING A LOT MORE CHALLENGING NOW NOW AS THE TRICKS BECOME TRICKIER.

READY TO LEARN HOW TO SPLIT THE ATOM?

STEP **1** Throw a **hard Long Sleeper.**

STEP **2** Take your other hand's **index finger** and raise it with the string.

89

STEP 3

Next, mount the yoyo by flipping it over to your throwhand's index finger. This is called a **"Split Bottom Mount."**

TAKE YOUR TIME TO PRACTICE AND MASTER THE SPLIT BOTTOM MOUNT BECAUSE THE NEXT FEW TRICKS WILL START FROM THIS MOVE.

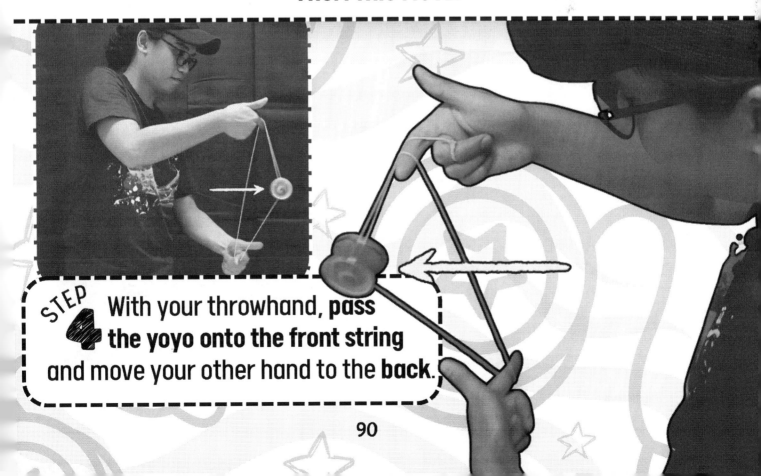

STEP 4

With your throwhand, **pass the yoyo onto the front string** and move your other hand to the **back**.

STEP 5

Push your **other hand's index finger forward** into the **two strings**.

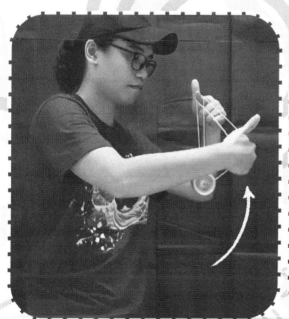

Then take your throwhand's index finger, passing **underneath the yoyo**, and **catch it on the same string**.

STEP 6 Using your throwhand, push into the strings **backward** and do **three flips**.

THIS PART IS SIMILAR TO THE BRAIN TWISTER TRICK MOVE.

TAKE A LOOK FROM A DIFFERENT ANGLE

FLIP IT THREE TIMES!

STOP!

RELEASE!

STEP 7 To complete the trick, take your throwhand's **finger out**

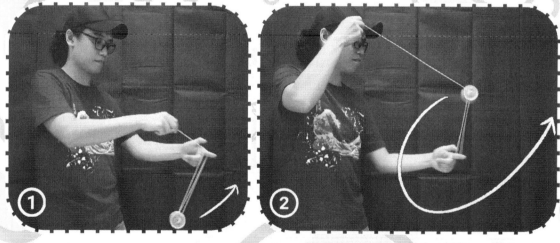

① ②

DISMOUNT THE YOYO, AND **RETURN** IT TO YOUR HAND.

③

MACH 5

TRICK NO. 27

NOW IT'S TIME TO **ACCELERATE** AND **REV UP** WITH THE **MACH 5** YOYO TRICK.

THIS ONE WILL IMPRESS EVERYONE, MAKING THE YOYO LOOK AS IF **IT'S FLOATING**.

STEP 1

Start with a **Long Sleeper**.

STEP 2

Perform a **Split Bottom Mount**

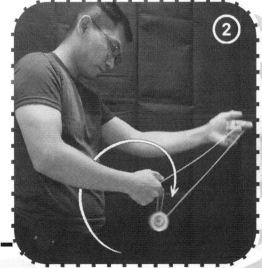

CHECK THE **SPLIT THE ATOM** TUTORIAL FOR GUIDANCE

STEP 3 Move your other hand **underneath the yoyo** and pass the yoyo onto the **front string.**

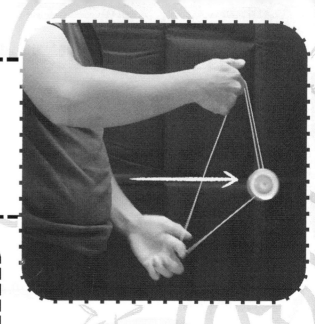

STEP 4 Then move your other hand **over your throwhand** and **back again underneath** it.

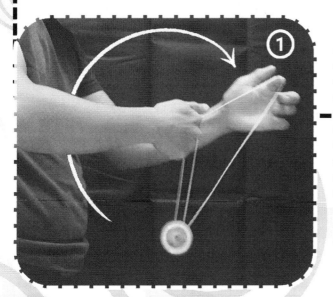
①

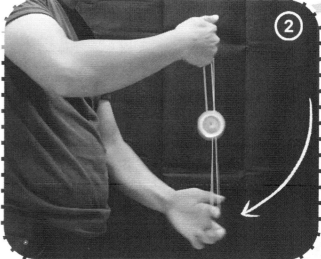
②

STEP 5 When your yoyo is in the middle, do a **rotating motion with both of your hands.**

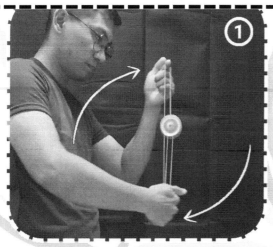
①

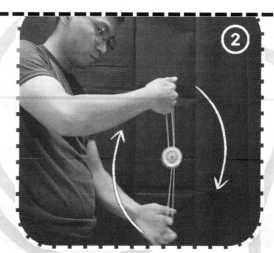
②

AS YOU ROTATE YOUR HANDS, YOUR YOYO WILL APPEAR TO BE FLOATING IN PLACE.

PERFORM THE ROTATION AT **LEAST THREE TIMES.**

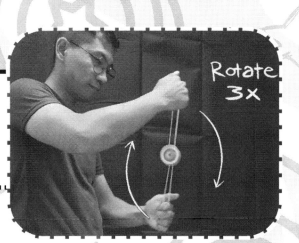

Rotate 3x

STEP 6

To finish, **remove your finger**, **dismount** the yoyo, and **catch** it.

① Release!

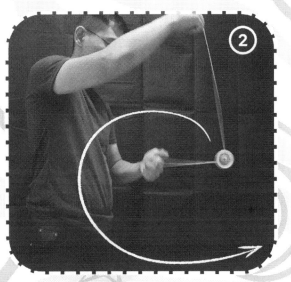

②

③

THIS TRICK IS PERFECT FOR IMPRESSING OTHERS, AS IT LOOKS LIKE YOU'RE DEFYING GRAVITY WITH YOUR YOYO!

ATOMIC FIRE

TRICK NO. 28

TIME TO BRING UP THE HEAT AND ELEVATE THE CHALLENGE FOR OUR NEXT TRICK - **ATOMIC FIRE.**

STEP 1 Start with a **Long Sleeper.**

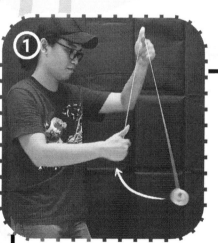

STEP 2 Perform a **Split Bottom Mount.**

With both hands, **do a somersault move** along with the yoyo.

TAKE A LOOK FROM A DIFFERENT ANGLE

Next, **push the yoyo onto the front string** while moving your **other hand's index finger** underneath the yoyo.

①

②

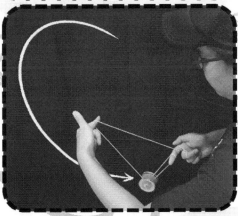

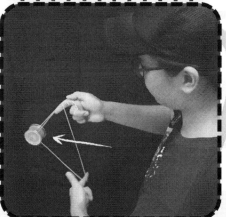

STEP 5 Move your **throwhand forward** and your other hand **backward**.

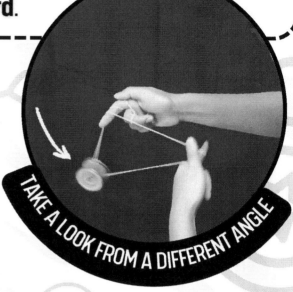

TAKE A LOOK FROM A DIFFERENT ANGLE

 STEP 6 **Flip the yoyo over** your throwhand's index finger onto the string and bring the yoyo back into the **Split Bottom Mount**.

Repeat the previous move twice or as many times as you can.

Lastly, **push the yoyo** onto the **front string** while moving your other hand **underneath** the yoyo, then **remove** your **throwhand's finger.**

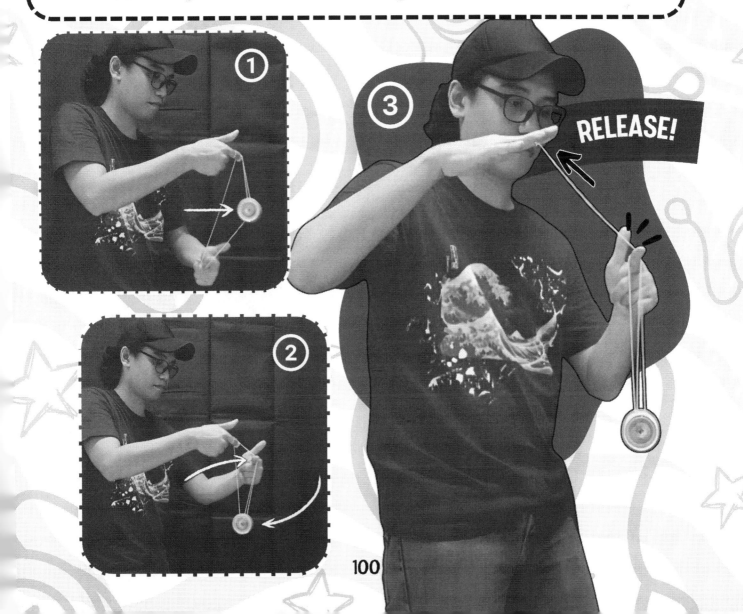

RELEASE!

STEP 9 **Dismount** the yoyo and **tug it back** to finish.

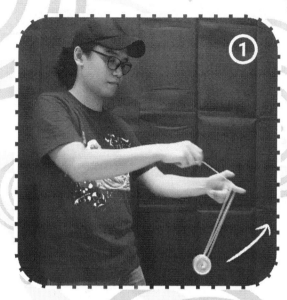

① ②

③

BASICALLY, YOU'RE DOING REPETITION MOVES IN ATOMIC FIRE BY **PASSING THE YOYO THROUGH THE STRING** AFTER YOU'VE DONE THE **SPLIT BOTTOM MOUNT** AND THE **SOMERSAULT.**

Tip LEARNING THE PREVIOUS TRICKS MAKES THIS ONE A WALK IN THE PARK.

BOINGY-BOINGY

TRICK NO. 29

TRICK NO. 29

LET'S MAKE THE YOYO BOUNCE BACK AND FORTH THIS TIME AS WE PERFORM THE **BOINGY-BOINGY TRICK!**

STEP 1 Start with a **Long Sleeper.**

STEP 2 Perform a **Split Bottom Mount.**

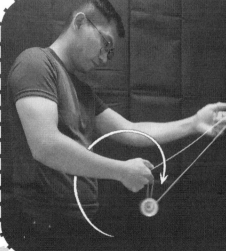

102

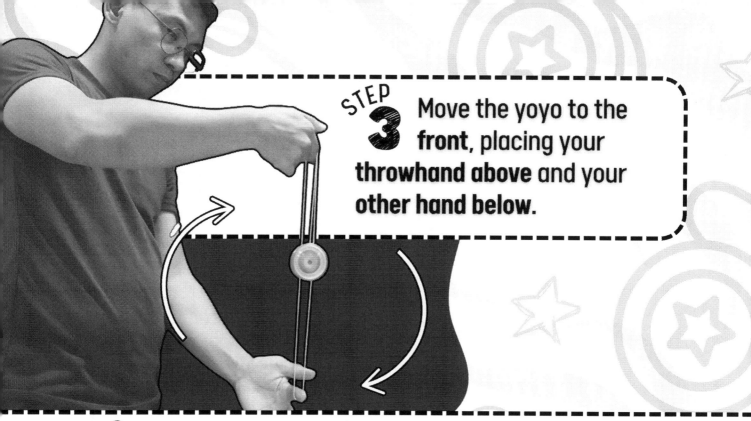

Move the yoyo to the **front**, placing your **throwhand above** and your **other hand below.**

STEP **4** The next step is to perform an **up-and-down motion** with your throwhand to **make the yoyo bounce back and forth.**

GO UP

AND DOWN

YOU MAY NOT GET THE MOVE RIGHT AWAY, BUT BE PATIENT AND TAKE YOUR TIME LEARNING IT.

BUT ONCE YOU GET IT, YOU CAN BOUNCE THE YOYO BACK AND FORTH AS MANY TIMES AS YOU WANT!

STEP 5

To finish, **pass** the yoyo **forward, dismount** it, and **catch** it in your hand.

① ② ③

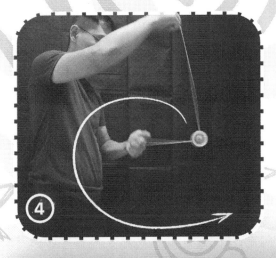

④ ⑤

NOW THAT YOU'VE MASTERED THE BOINGY-BOINGY TRICK, **YOU'RE FINALLY READY** FOR OUR FINAL TRICK IN THE ADVANCED LEVEL.

ELI HOP

THE ELI HOP TRICK MAY LOOK SIMPLE. IT'S JUST A TRAPEZE, THEN A HOP INTO THE AIR AND BACK TO TRAPEZE AGAIN. BUT DON'T BE FOOLED! THERE'S A REASON WHY THIS IS THE FINAL TRICK. DON'T WORRY, WE'LL SHOW YOU HOW TO DO IT.

 STEP 1 Throw a **Breakaway** to make a **Trapeze**.

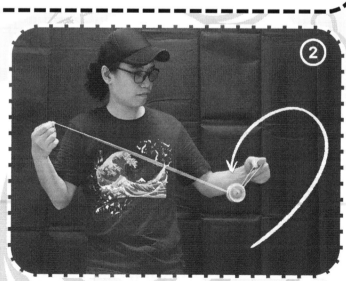

STEP 2 **Position** the yoyo **below** and **pull the string up** to make the yoyo **hop** into the air.

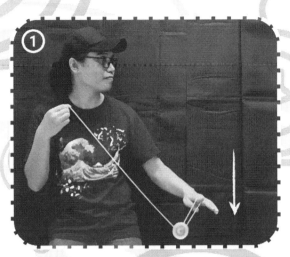

AS YOU PERFORM THE HOP, BRING BOTH OF YOUR HANDS CLOSER TOGETHER TO CONTROL THE YOYO'S MOVEMENT.

Your **throwhand does the pulling** to make the yoyo hop, while your **other hand assists**.

Also, the other hand touches the string to keep the yoyo on track.

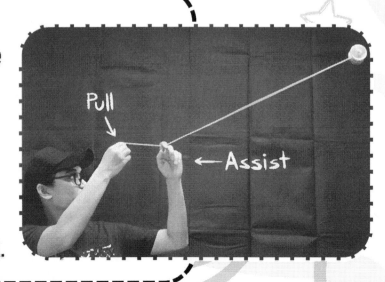

Pull

← Assist

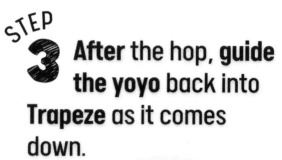

STEP 3 After the hop, **guide the yoyo** back into **Trapeze** as it comes down.

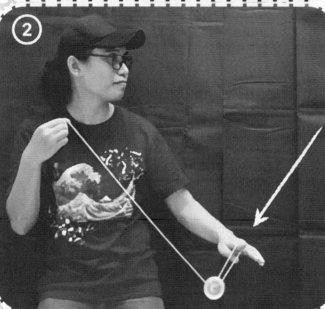

CONTROL IS THE KEY FOR THIS TRICK, AND MAKE SURE YOUR STRING IS ALIGNED SO YOU DON'T MISS THE LANDING.

3x

STEP 4 Do the hop at **least three times** (or as many times as you want).

STEP 5 Finish the trick by **popping** the yoyo **out of Trapeze** and returning it to your hand.

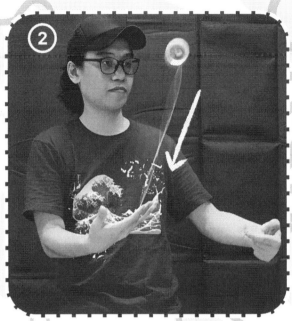

WHILE ELI HOP MAY NOT BE AS COMPLEX AS SOME STRING TRICKS, IT'S MUCH TRICKIER.

BUT WITH PATIENCE, MASTERING IT WILL BRING GREAT SATISFACTION.

CONGRATULATIONS!

YOU'VE COMPLETED THE ADVANCED LEVEL.

THIS WAS NO EASY FEAT, BUT YOU'VE MANAGED TO LEARN ALL THE TRICKS AND HAVE BECOME

A TRUE YOYO MASTER

READY TO LEARN HOW TO DO

THE DNA TRICK?

CLAIM YOUR **FREE BONUS VIDEO TUTORIAL & PDF** BY SCANNING THE QR CODE BELOW*

*SELECT 'FREE PREVIEW' TO ACCESS THIS BONUS

THERE YOU HAVE IT, FOLKS!

WE'VE MADE IT TO THE END OF THIS YOYO TRICK BOOK, AND WE ARE INCREDIBLY PROUD OF YOU!

WE HOPE THAT YOUR YOYO JOURNEY CONTINUES AND THAT YOU SHARE THE FUN OF YOYOING WITH MANY OTHERS!

WITH THE TRICKS YOU'VE LEARNED, NOW IS THE TIME TO GET CREATIVE AND START CRAFTING YOUR OWN ORIGINAL YOYO TRICKS.

111

UNLOCK YOUR ADVENTURE

By scanning the QR code or following the link below, you'll step into an **interactive escape room** designed just for you. Solve puzzles, unlock secrets, and navigate through a maze of mystery — all in a race against time.

Your adventure awaits. Dare to unlock it?

bit.ly/4Opw6Lz

Get FREE access to a BONUS BOOK OF RIDDLES!

TRICKY RIDDLES FOR KIDS

EXTRA BONUS

300+ RIDDLES!

NO SIGN-UP REQUIRED!

SCAN THE QR CODE TO START YOUR RIDDLE ADVENTURE!

PERFECT FOR ALL AGES
Fun for kids, adults, & families.

ALL SKILL LEVELS
Easy, difficult, and insanely hard riddles included.

VARIETY OF CATEGORIES
From animals and space to detective challenges.

INTERACTIVE CREATIVITY
Includes a section to create your own riddles!

Made in the USA
Las Vegas, NV
13 December 2024

14049081R00063